AMAZING REPTILES
and AMPHIBIANS

By Brian Williams

Gareth Stevens
Publishing

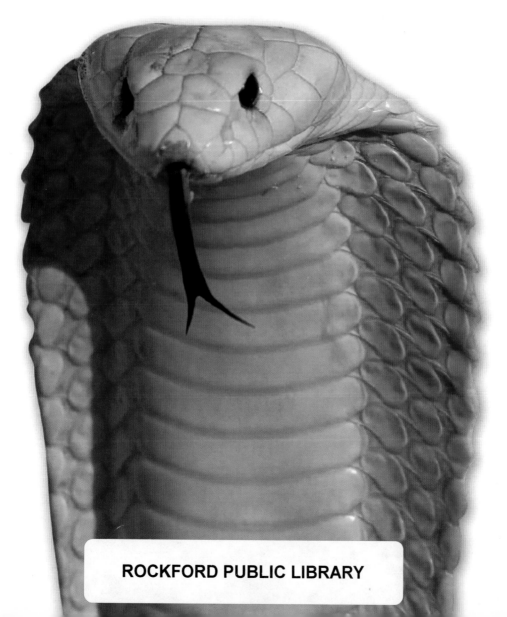

Please visit our web site at www.garethstevens.com.
For a free catalog describing our list of high-quality books, call 1-800-542-2595 (USA)
or 1-800-387-3178 (Canada). Our fax: 1-877-542-2596

Library of Congress Cataloging-in-Publication Data
Williams, Brian, 1943–
     Amazing reptiles and amphibians / Brian Williams.
       p. cm. — (Amazing life cycles)
     Includes index.
     ISBN-13: 978-0-8368-8898-0 (lib. bdg.)
     ISBN-10: 0-8368-8898-7 (lib. bdg.)
     1. Reptiles—Juvenile literature. 2. Reptiles—Life cycles—Juvenile
literature. 3. Amphibians—Juvenile literature. 4. Amphibians—Life
cycles—Juvenile literature. I. Title.
QL644.2.W595   2008
597.9—dc22   2007043756

This North American edition first published in 2008 by
Gareth Stevens Publishing
A Weekly Reader® Company
1 Reader's Digest Road
Pleasantville, NY 10570-7000 USA

This U.S. edition copyright © 2008 by Gareth Stevens, Inc. Original edition copyright © 2007 by ticktock Media Ltd.
First published in Great Britain in 2007 by ticktock Media Ltd., Unit 2, Orchard Business Centre, North Farm Road,
Tunbridge Wells, Kent, TN2 3XF United Kingdom

ticktock Project Editor: Ruth Owen
ticktock Project Designer: Sara Greasley
With thanks to: Trudi Webb, Sally Morgan, and Elizabeth Wiggans

Gareth Stevens Senior Editor: Brian Fitzgerald
Gareth Stevens Creative Director: Lisa Donovan
Gareth Stevens Graphic Designer: Alex Davis
With thanks to: Mark Sachner

Photo credits (t = top; b = bottom; c = center; l = left; r = right):
FLPA: 4b, 5t, 6b, 7b, 11b, 17t, 18cl, 25t, 25b, 26–27 all. Nature Picture Library: 16b, 19t, 23t, 29t. NHPA: 28–29, 31t.
Shutterstock: cover, title page, contents page, 4c, 6t, 8tl, 8b, 9t, 9c, 9b, 10tl, 10 main, 12tl, 13c, 13b, 14–15 all, 20 all, 22tl,
22–23 main, 24tl, 24–25 main, 30tl, 31b. Superstock: 5b, 8c, 11t, 13t, 16tl, 17b, 18tl, 19b, 21t, 21b, 30b. Ticktock image archive:
4tl, 7t, map page 12.

Every effort has been made to trace copyright holders, and we apologize in advance for any omissions. We would be
pleased to insert the appropriate acknowledgments in any subsequent edition of this publication.

Printed in the United States of America

1 2 3 4 5 6 7 8 9 10 09 08 07

Contents

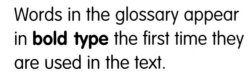

Words in the glossary appear in **bold type** the first time they are used in the text.

What Is a Reptile?

A reptile is an animal with thick skin covered in **scales**. Reptiles are **cold-blooded**. Their body temperature goes up or down with the temperature of the air or water around them.

A crocodile's foot is covered with scaly skin.

Snakes, lizards, crocodiles, alligators, tortoises, and turtles are all reptiles.

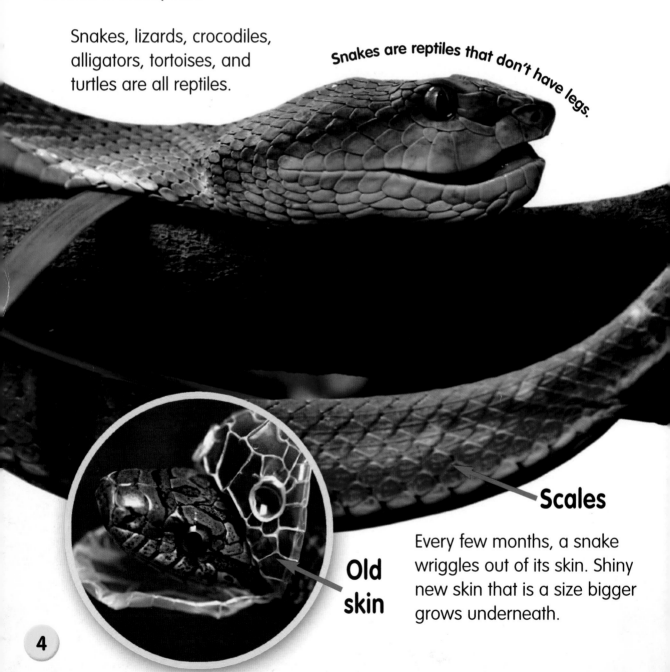

Snakes are reptiles that don't have legs.

Scales

Old skin

Every few months, a snake wriggles out of its skin. Shiny new skin that is a size bigger grows underneath.

Lizards are reptiles. Most lizards have four legs and a tail.

If a bird or some other **predator** grabs a lizard's tail, the tip breaks off. The predator is left with the twitching part of the tail. The lizard runs away and soon grows a new tail!

AMAZING REPTILE FACT
Giant Galápagos tortoises can live to be more than 100 years old.

This lizard is growing a new tail. The tip is missing!

Tortoises and turtles are reptiles that have hard shells. The shell protects them from predators.

A giant Galápagos tortoise

Reptile Life

Adult reptiles usually live on their own. Males and females get together to **mate** and then go separate ways. After mating, most female reptiles lay eggs, but some reptiles give birth to live babies.

The emerald tree boa gives birth to live babies.

Chameleons are tree lizards that can change their skin color! The female shows the male she is ready to mate by changing color.

AMAZING REPTILE FACT
Reptile eggs feel rubbery. The shell is strong but softer than a bird's egg.

Male chameleons are larger than females.

Female

Male

Reptiles lay many eggs at a time. Only a few **hatch**. The rest are often eaten by other animals.

Female pythons coil their bodies around their eggs to keep them warm.

Most reptile moms leave their eggs to hatch on their own, but some stay close to protect their eggs.

When a baby reptile hatches, it looks like a tiny copy of its parents. The baby is ready to find its own food right away. Baby snakes can hunt as soon as they are born.

This western pond turtle has just hatched.

Egg

What Is an Amphibian?

An amphibian is an animal that lives in water and on land. Like reptiles, amphibians are cold-blooded. Their bodies are about the same temperature as the air or water around them. Amphibians have smooth skin.

A toad looks like a frog, but it has drier, bumpier skin.

Salamanders, frogs, toads, newts, and caecilians (Sih-SILL-yens) are all amphibians.

Newts and salamanders are amphibians that have tails.

The caecilian looks like a worm or a snake.

A fire salamander can squirt a poisonous fluid at predators.

AMAZING AMPHIBIAN FACT
The word amphibian means "two lives"—one on land and one in water.

Most amphibians like warm, damp places that have plenty of plants they can use for hiding.

Frogs and toads are amphibians that have no tails.

The bright blue color of the poison dart frog tells predators, "Stay away! I'm poisonous!"

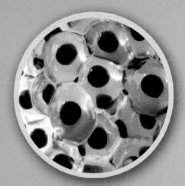

Amphibian eggs
have no shells. Frog
eggs look like jelly!

Amphibian Life

Adult amphibians usually live on their own.
Males and females get together to mate.
After mating, female amphibians lay eggs.
Most amphibians lay their eggs in water to
keep the eggs from drying out.

In spring, male and female frogs
and toads gather in ponds to mate.
Then the females lay eggs.

**AMAZING
AMPHIBIAN FACT**
Male frogs puff out their
throats to let out a deep,
croaky call. This call
attracts females.

Baby amphibians hatch from eggs. They have large heads and long tails. They breathe through **gills**, like fish do. As they grow, they develop legs and lungs. Then they can live on land.

These are the babies of a spotted salamander.

Most amphibians don't look after their eggs or babies, but some amphibians are amazing parents!

Some poison dart frogs lay their eggs in water-filled hollows in trees. After the eggs hatch, the frogs carry the **tadpoles** to a new home if the water dries out.

Eggs

The male midwife toad carries his eggs on his back until they hatch.

Animal Habitats

A **habitat** is the place where a plant or an animal lives. Reptiles and amphibians live in lots of habitats, from warm, wet tropical rain forests to dry grasslands. Many amphibians live in ponds and rivers in wetlands.

The sea is a habitat. Turtles live in the sea.

Reptiles and amphibians live in all habitats except Antarctica and the Arctic.

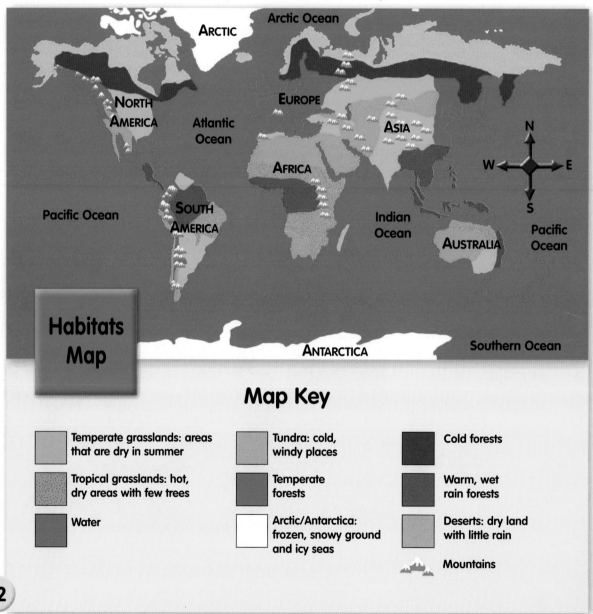

ARCTIC

Arctic Ocean

EUROPE

NORTH AMERICA

Atlantic Ocean

ASIA

AFRICA

N

W — E

S

Pacific Ocean

SOUTH AMERICA

Indian Ocean

Pacific Ocean

AUSTRALIA

Habitats Map

ANTARCTICA

Southern Ocean

Map Key

	Temperate grasslands: areas that are dry in summer
	Tropical grasslands: hot, dry areas with few trees
	Water

	Tundra: cold, windy places
	Temperate forests
	Arctic/Antarctica: frozen, snowy ground and icy seas

	Cold forests
	Warm, wet rain forests
	Deserts: dry land with little rain
	Mountains

12

Many snakes and lizards live in deserts, which can be cold at night. In the morning, they lie in the Sun to warm up their bodies.

A marine iguana

The thorny devil lizard lives in deserts in Australia.

This tree frog's green color helps it blend in with the leaves.

Marine iguanas are reptiles that live on beaches and rocky shores. Adult marine iguanas dive in the ocean to find food.

Tree frogs live in forest habitats. Their skin color acts as **camouflage** that helps them hide from predators and the insects they hunt.

AMAZING REPTILE FACT
There are more than 1,000 different kinds of tree frogs.

What Is a Life Cycle?

A **life cycle** is the different stages that an animal or a plant goes through in its life. The diagrams on these pages show the usual life cycles of reptiles and amphibians.

The male Jackson's chameleon uses his horns to fight other males for females.

A pair of rattlesnakes

1

A male and a female snake meet and mate.

A young emerald tree boa

4

Baby snakes are ready to go off on their own as soon as they hatch or are born.

SNAKE LIFE CYCLE
All reptiles have a life cycle with these stages.

A female corn snake

2

The female lays eggs. Some snakes give birth to live babies.

A baby ball python

3

Baby snakes hatch from the eggs.

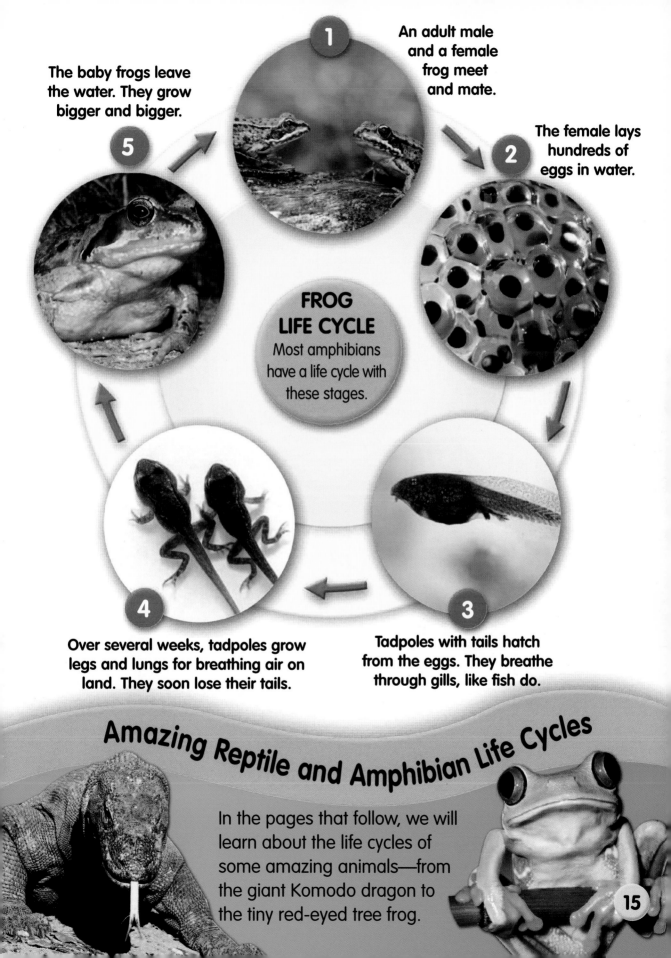

1 An adult male and a female frog meet and mate.

2 The female lays hundreds of eggs in water.

The baby frogs leave the water. They grow bigger and bigger.

5

FROG LIFE CYCLE
Most amphibians have a life cycle with these stages.

4 Over several weeks, tadpoles grow legs and lungs for breathing air on land. They soon lose their tails.

3 Tadpoles with tails hatch from the eggs. They breathe through gills, like fish do.

Amazing Reptile and Amphibian Life Cycles

In the pages that follow, we will learn about the life cycles of some amazing animals—from the giant Komodo dragon to the tiny red-eyed tree frog.

15

Egg-Eating Snake

The egg-eating snake lives on grasslands and in deserts in Africa. The snake has no teeth, but it can swallow a bird's egg that is bigger than its own head!

An egg-eating snake can grow to 3 feet (1 meter) in length.

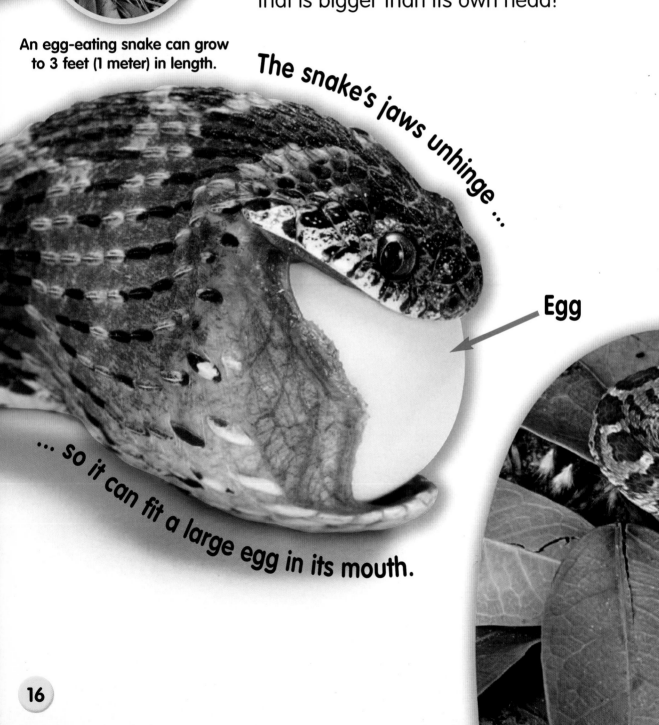

The snake's jaws unhinge ...

Egg

... so it can fit a large egg in its mouth.

As the snake swallows, its skin stretches around the egg.

The egg-eating snake has sharp spikes inside its throat to crack the eggshell. The snake swallows the yolk and white, and spits out the shell.

A female egg-eating snake lays from 6 to 25 eggs. She scatters them around her area and then leaves them. The eggs hatch after two to three months.

Young egg-eaters climb trees to look for eggs.

AMAZING REPTILE FACT

Before eating an egg, the snake touches it with its tongue to make sure it is fresh.

Crocodiles can bite, but they cannot chew.

Nile Crocodile

The Nile crocodile lives beside lakes and rivers in Africa. It waits for a large animal, such as an antelope, to come for a drink. Then the crocodile grabs its **prey** and eats it! Nile crocodiles also eat monkeys, turtles, birds, and fish.

After mating, the female crocodile makes a nest beside the river. She lays 50 to 60 eggs. The eggs hatch after about 60 days.

Newly hatched babies head straight from the nest to their mom!

Baby crocodile

Crocodiles are fierce, but they are very good moms. They guard their eggs from predators. They even help break open the eggs with their mouths so the babies can get out.

AMAZING REPTILE FACT
A male Nile crocodile can grow to nearly 20 feet (6 m) long.

This baby crocodile is about to call to its mom to let her know it has hatched.

The female looks after its babies in the shallow water of the river. After about eight weeks, the babies go off on their own.

The female gently carries her babies from the nest to the river in her mouth.

An adult green turtle weighs up to 450 pounds (200 kilograms).

Green Sea Turtle

The green sea turtle lives in warm oceans. Green turtles eat underwater plants, such as sea grass. Female green turtles go to the same beach every year to mate and lay eggs.

AMAZING REPTILE FACT

Some females swim more than 600 miles (1,000 kilometers) to get to their breeding beach.

Adult male and female turtles meet and mate in shallow water.

Flipper

Turtles swim by paddling with their flippers.

After mating in shallow water, females return to the beach.

After mating, the female turtle crawls up the beach. She digs a deep hole in the sand with her flippers. She lays her eggs, covers them with sand, and crawls back to the sea.

The green turtle lays up to 200 eggs at one time.

The baby turtles hatch after about seven weeks. The babies have to look after themselves. They dig out of the sand and crawl as quickly as they can to the sea.

The tiny turtle hatchlings are in danger of being eaten by seabirds and other predators.

The Komodo dragon's saliva is full of germs. Just one bite can kill its prey.

Komodo Dragon

The Komodo dragon is the world's largest lizard. These giant reptiles live on Komodo Island and other islands in Indonesia, a nation in Southeast Asia. Komodo dragons hunt for wild pigs and deer. They also eat animals that are already dead.

Male Komodos stand on their back legs to fight over who gets to mate with a female.

An adult male can be 10 feet (3 m) long!

After mating, the female digs a shallow nest in the ground and lays about 25 eggs. She then leaves the eggs to hatch on their own.

The dragon's eggs hatch after seven to nine months. The babies climb trees and eat insects and lizards. Baby Komodo dragons are safe in the treetops from predators. That includes adult Komodo dragons, which eat baby dragons!

This baby Komodo dragon is two days old and about 1 foot (30 centimeters) long.

AMAZING REPTILE FACT
A female Komodo dragon in a British zoo laid eggs that hatched into babies—even though she never mated with a male!

Red-Eyed Tree Frog

The red-eyed tree frog lives in rain forests in Central America. It is a **nocturnal** frog. This means it rests during the day and is active at night. Red-eyed tree frogs eat insects.

A frog's toes have suction pads to help the frog stick to leaves.

During mating season, male red-eyed tree frogs gather on branches over a pond.

AMAZING AMPHIBIAN FACT
With its eyes closed, the frog blends into its green habitat. If attacked, the frog startles predators by opening its big red eyes.

The males call to females with a clicking noise.

After mating, the female lays up to 50 eggs on a leaf hanging over the pond. Laying lots of eggs at a time means at least some babies will survive. Snakes and other predators feed on frog eggs.

After these tadpoles have grown into frogs, they will climb back into the trees.

After about five days, the eggs hatch and the tadpoles fall down into the pond below. Tadpoles develop into frogs in about 75 days.

Tadpole

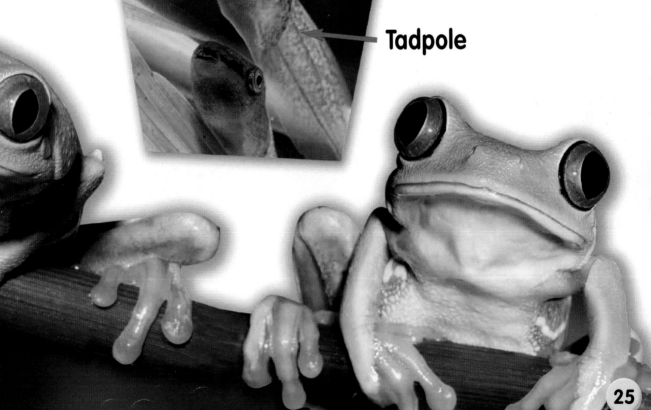

A Darwin's frog can
wiggle its pointy nose
back and forth.

Darwin's Frog

The Darwin's frog lives near rivers in damp, shady mountain forests in South America. Darwin's frogs eat worms, other insects, and small animals. The males are good fathers.

After a female Darwin's frog has laid her eggs, the male guards them. In about two weeks, the babies inside the eggs start to move. The male then picks up the eggs with his tongue and puts them into a pouch in his mouth. He can fit up to 15 eggs in his mouth at one time.

The eggs are in here!

The tadpoles hatch inside the male's mouth. They stay in his mouth for 50 days and feed on their own egg yolks. Once they have grown into little froglets, the babies climb out of dad's mouth!

An adult Darwin's frog is only about 1 inch (2.5 cm) long.

Froglet

If an axolotl loses a leg, it can grow another one.

Axolotl

The axolotl is an amphibian that looks like a baby even when it is an adult. It is a kind of salamander, but it looks like a giant tadpole. Axolotls live in lakes in Mexico, but people also keep them as pets. Some people like to eat axolotls!

The axolotl breathes through gills not lungs. It never comes out of the water.

The axolotl is about 10 inches (25 cm) long.

Gills

Axolotls mate in water. After mating, the female lays up to 1,000 eggs and sticks them to underwater plants and stones.

The eggs hatch in two to three weeks. The babies eat tiny water animals. The axolotl's legs start to grow after about 10 days.

Baby axolotls look a lot like their parents.

Tail

AMAZING AMPHIBIAN FACT
Baby axolotls sometimes eat each other!

That's Amazing!

Reptiles and amphibians are some of the most stunning creatures on Earth. They come in many sizes. So do their babies! Reptiles and amphibians are born or hatched in a lot of unusual ways.

The North American bullfrog lays 25,000 eggs at a time.

Several people are needed to carry an anaconda.

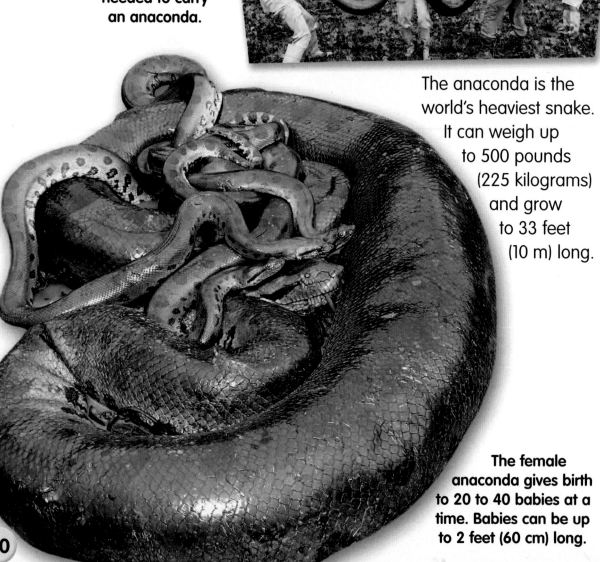

The anaconda is the world's heaviest snake. It can weigh up to 500 pounds (225 kilograms) and grow to 33 feet (10 m) long.

The female anaconda gives birth to 20 to 40 babies at a time. Babies can be up to 2 feet (60 cm) long.

The Surinam toad's life cycle does not include tadpoles. The female Surinam toad lays her eggs, and the male puts them on her back. A protective covering of skin grows over the eggs. When the eggs hatch, baby toads break through the skin.

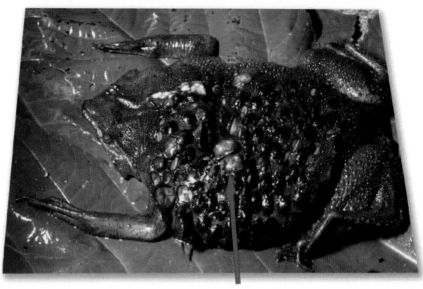

Eggs and baby toads

The tuatara is in a reptile family all its own. Its closest relatives lived among the dinosaurs during prehistoric times.

AMAZING REPTILE FACT
When resting, tuataras may take only one breath an hour!

Baby tuataras take up to 15 months to hatch from their eggs. No other reptile takes as long.

Glossary

camouflage: colors, marks, or a shape that hides an animal from predators and its prey

cold-blooded: describes an animal whose body temperature goes up or down depending on how hot or cold the air or water is around it

gills: breathing organs in animals that live in water, such as fish and baby amphibians

habitat: the natural conditions in which a plant or an animal lives

hatch: to break out of an egg

life cycle: the series of changes that an animal or a plant goes through in its life

mate: to come together to make eggs or babies

nocturnal: active at night

predator: an animal that hunts and kills other animals for food

prey: animals that are hunted by other animals as food

scales: hard plates of skin that cover the bodies of reptiles and fish

tadpoles: young frogs or toads that have not yet developed lungs

Index